Stay
on the
Potter's
Wheel

Dr. David A. "Garmon" Jordan Sr.

WESTBOW
PRESS®
A DIVISION OF THOMAS NELSON
& ZONDERVAN

Scripture taken from the King James Version of the Bible.

Scripture quotations taken from the Holy Bible, New Living Translation, Copyright © 1996, 2004. Used by permission of Tyndale House Publishers, Inc., Wheaton, Illinois 60189. All rights reserved.

WestBow Press books may be ordered through booksellers or by contacting:

WestBow Press
A Division of Thomas Nelson & Zondervan
1663 Liberty Drive
Bloomington, IN 47403
www.westbowpress.com
1 (866) 928-1240

Because of the dynamic nature of the Internet, any web addresses or links contained in this book may have changed since publication and may no longer be valid. The views expressed in this work are solely those of the author and do not necessarily reflect the views of the publisher, and the publisher hereby disclaims any responsibility for them.

Any people depicted in stock imagery provided by Thinkstock are models, and such images are being used for illustrative purposes only. Certain stock imagery © Thinkstock.

ISBN: 978-1-9736-0690-1 (sc)
ISBN: 978-1-9736-0691-8 (hc)
ISBN: 978-1-9736-0689-5 (e)

Library of Congress Control Number: 2017917295

Print information available on the last page.

WestBow Press rev. date: 12/06/2017

God is not Finished with You Yet!!
Stay on the Potter's Wheel

Contents

About the Author

In 1954, I was born into this world and named David Allen (Garmon) Jordan, Sr. I was born in Hayti, Missouri, the son of Willie C. Garmon, who was a share cropper, and Almeda "Davis" Garmon, who worked chopping and picking cotton. Today, I am a grown God-fearing preacher who preaches and teaches.

I've learned how to stand on the Word of God and listen to what "He" God is telling me in the Spirit. It's still a spiritual battle. Through many ups and down, falls and failures, I have learned to stand on the promises of God, and to stay on the Potter's wheel.

I met my beautiful wife Carla, and we got married in 1993 in St. Louis, Missouri. We moved to North Carolina where we resided for 11 years; together, we have six beautiful children.

My son, David Jr., was born weighing only 2 pound 12 ounces. God began to use me to stand, not on what I knew, but what He was doing in my life. My wife and I had some hard times in our marriage, and if not for the hand of God moving in our lives and standing on the Potter's wheel, we wouldn't be together today.

While we may have gone through things in our life, with the ups and downs, we were learning how we must stand on the Potter's wheel and not jump off. Because we trust in God, He has made ways out of nothing for us.

God blessed Carla and me with four beautiful daughters, Cosandra, LaTisha, Myra Alexandria, and Michala Grace, and two handsome sons, Joshua and David Jr. They all have been an inspiration and a blessing to me.

I believe that God has directed me to write this book so others may be helped by hearing my testimony, and how God has brought us out.

We were made in the image of God and He wants the best for us. So, to understand our parts, we must read and study God's word and pray. The main things are to stand on the Potter's wheel and not jump off!

Thanks

I want to thank God for giving me the opportunity to write this book. I pray that it will be a blessing to those who need it and are open to His word.

To my wife, Carla, and my six children, Cosandra, LaTisha, Joshua, David Jr, Myra, Michala, for their encouragement of me with this project. Thank all of you!!!!!!!

Thanks to Andre Williams, of EAZYYOKEART, for doing the great art work, and working with me to put the idea I have together.

I want to thank Dr. Lonetta Oliver for editing my book, she was a great help. God bless all of you.

1

What is the Potter's wheel?

A Potter's Wheel is a machine used to shape clay into a vessel to be used as the potter shapes the clay. The wheel is used to turn the clay so it can be shaped in the way or into the image the potter wants it to become.

The Potter's Wheel was used throughout the old world to make items for their food and drink. Pottery was handmade and included items such as cups and bowls and involved methods that required special equipment, which included the coiling and turntable.

It is not known when the potter's wheel was invented, but I am starting with where God was using Jeremiah to give us the message, around 612 B.C.

The Potter shapes the clay into be the vessel so it can be used in whatever way he or she wants to use it.

Jeremiah 18:6, we see where God is concerned about us and He wants the best for us and out of us.

From Adam and Eve until now, God has been trying to help and show man how to be in His image. He allows us to be on the Potter's wheel so we can understand what He "God" wants us to be. When we look through the Bible, we see that God loves mankind so much that He goes to unmeasured, unlimited lengths trying to make man see it.

Sometime the clay had to be broken up into pieces and crumbled up so it can be reused. We go through things; sometimes we do it right and sometimes we don't, but God loves us so much, and is so faithful towards us that He takes time with us to see if we will get it right.

Lamentations 3: 22-25

As the Potters would make vessels so they could be used to put food, water or whatever they were needed for, God puts us on the Potter's wheel to mold and make us in his image so He can use us according to His will.

Notes

Notes

Notes

2

God's People on the Potter's Wheel

It is so important to know who we are in the Lord. So many are saved, but "God's" people don't realize who they are. They are saved, but don't know God personally. We need to know Him intimately and love Him with all our hearts.

God is not there to hurt us, but to get us to trust Him. Yes, sometimes we may have to go through some hard times, but God is there to help us if we just put our trust in Him. All through the Bible we see that God uses prophets, teachers, men, women boys and girls to show us that He loves us and wants the best out of our lives.

As people of God, we want to be able to show others how we went through hardships, downfalls and mistreatment, but also how we keep the faith and stay on the Potter's wheel. Men were killed thrown into prison, women were raped children were sold, and God used them to bring some hope for us.

In the book of Jeremiah, we read that God had Jeremiah go down to the Potter's house. In **Jeremiah 18:1-6**, the word which came to Jeremiah from the Lord said, "Arise, and go down to the Potter's house, and there I will cause thee to hear my words."

"Then I went down to the Potter's house, and, behold, He wrought a work on the wheels. And the vessel that He made of clay was marred in the hand of the Potter's: so He made it again another vessel, as seemed good to the Potter's to make it.

Then the word of the Lord came to me, saying, O house of Israel, cannot I do with you as this Potter's? saith the Lord. Behold, as the clay is in the Potter's hand, so are ye in mine hand, O house of Israel." God was letting him know that He can do what He wants in our lives, because He made us, and is trying to use us in his will, not our will.

The Potter's wheel sometimes means temptation, heartache, and downfalls. We stay on the wheel so God can mold us into his image, and that his will be done in our lives. We get scarred, scraped, and have some bleeding sometimes, but God knows all of that.

Yes, these things happen to us, but we need to stay on the wheel because God is not finished with us yet. God is trying to make us complete so we will be able to help others.

Many times, when we are going through difficult times we get depressed, and feel like we can't go on with life. We want to give up. Instead, we must trust in the Lord, and stay on the Potter's wheel so He can help us through these times.

James 1:2, "My brethren, count is all joy when ye fall into divers' temptations; knowing this, that the trying of your faith worketh patience. But let patience have Her prefect work that ye may be perfect and entire, wanting nothing.

Jeremiah was on the Potter's wheel of the dungeon and cistern. God allowed Him to be put in a dungeon and cistern, not because of what Jeremiah had done but, because God wanted to use him. Even if we are down below the earth, He is able to deliver us from it.

You see, it is not what we are going through, but how we deal with the situations that we're in. Our attitude has a lot to do with how we grow in the Lord. We must learn how to love people and treat them in a respectful way.

Daniel and the Hebrew boys, Shadrach, Meshach,

and Abednego, were on the Potter's wheel in their various situations.

Daniel 6:16-22, Daniel was placed in the lion's and his faith protected Him from the bite from the lions. God shut up the lion's mouth. And because of that Daniel was protected. He stays on the wheel until God was finish with Him.

Due to lies and jealousy of others, Daniel was place in the lion's den. Then the king commanded his people, and said to bring Daniel. They cast Him into the den of lions. Now the king spoke and said unto Daniel, Thy God whom thou Servest continually, He will deliver thee.

Daniel 6:19-21, At the first light of dawn, the king got up and hurried to the lions' den. When he came near the den, he called to Daniel in an anguished voice, "Daniel, servant of the living God, has your God, whom you serve continually, been able to rescue you from the lions?"

Daniel answered, "May the king live forever!

Daniel 3:11-25, We see that we must go against the odds to stay on the wheel, and we must trust in the Lord.

There was an order from the King to bow down and worship him. It was a decree that would cause anyone who refused to be placed in a fiery furnace.

Shadrach, Meshach, and Abednego were placed over the affairs of the province of Babylon, but would not serve the King's gods, nor worship the golden idol which He had set up. They were placed in the fiery furnace because of what they believed in, and stayed on the Potter's wheel, waiting for God to deliver them.

Nebuchadnezzar the king was astonished, and rose up in haste. He spoke unto his counselors, 'Did not we cast three men bound into the mist of the fire?' They answered and said unto the king true, O king. He answers and said, 'Lo, I see four men loose, walking in the midst, of the fire, and they have no hurt; and the form of the fourth is like the Son of God.'

Do you know what the Son of God looks like; and in your situation, can you trust His will enough to stay on the wheel so that you can be delivered?

In our lives, we all have a lion's den, and furnaces of fire we are going through. We all have some rugged valley to walk through, or a rough mountain to climb. That's why we must stay on the Potter's wheel because we can't make it on our own.

During difficult times, we need to be strong, and have the courage and faith to stand the tests that we are in, so God can get the glory out of our lives.

Hebrew 11:1-41, We see patriarchs; they had faith to stand on the Potter's wheel.

They left us with the promise that we can make it if we put our trust in God, and stay on the Potter's wheel. If we don't jump off, we can do all things through Christ that gives us strength.

Who are God's people? God's people are those who are saved, and have given our lives to Him. We are those who are born again, washed by His blood. God owns every human, but only those of us that trust in the Lord are His.

St. John 10:1-5 Verily, verily, I say unto to you, He that entered not by the door into the sheep fold, but climbed up some other way, the same is a thief and a robber. But He that entered in by the door is the shepherd of the sheep.

To Him the porter opened; and He call his own sheep Hear his voice: and He called his own sheep by name, and lead them out. And when He putted forth his own sheep, He goes before them, and the sheep follow Him.

And stranger will they not follow, but will flee from: for they know not the voice of a strangers. God's people have gotten so weak, that we allow anything to influence us to do what the world do.

We must take back the terror that Satan have taken from us, by stand on the word of God, and do as He (God) would have us to do.

Notes

Notes

Notes

3

God is in Control

Since the beginning of time, after Adam and Eve sinned, God has been trying to bring mankind back to a relationship with Him. God drove Adam and Eve out of the garden, and placed Cherubim, angels with a flaming sword which turned every way, to keep them away from the Tree of Life. This was to protect them, so they would not eat of the Tree of Life and live in sin for eternity. Just think if they had eaten of the tree, we would have any way to salvation, because they would forfeit it all.

God loves all of us, even in all our messes. God looks beyond all of our faults, and sees the need to help us. Remember that He is always in control, no matter what we think or feel, and we need Him to take our hand and lead us to victory.

We need to listen to what God is saying to us. Not just with our natural ears but, we must ask God to open our spiritual ears.

Revelation 2: 7, He that hath an ear, let Him Hear what the Spirit saith unto the churches; to Him that overcomes will I give to eat of the tree of life, which is in the mist of the paradise of God.

While we go through what we are having our trails, we just trust in God to take us through, and give that we may give the praise and the glory, because He is in control of our lives.

When Jesus was in the garden of Gethsemane, **St. Matthew.26:39-42,** and He went a litter farther, and fell on his face, and prayed, saying O my Father, if it be possible, let this cup pass from me; nevertheless, not as I will, but a though wilt. And He cometh the disciple, and fined them asleep, and saith unto Peter, What! Could ye not watch with me one hour?

Watch and pray that ye enter not into temptation: the spirit indeed is willing, but the flesh is weak. He went away again the second time, and prayed, saying. O my Father, if this cup may not pass away from me, except I drink it thy will be done. Here we that Jesus submitted Himself to God. We must submit ourselves to God so He can have control of our lives. **James 4:7**

Submit yourself therefore to God Resist the devil, and He will flee from you.

Remember that we can't fight the devil on our own. Without Him, we will lose the battle, and possibly our lives too.

1 Samuel 17: 47, And all this assembly shall know that the Lord saveth not with sword and spear: for the battle is the Lord's and He will give you into our hands.

God wants to be in complete control of our lives, because we were bought with a price, and that is the blood of Jesus. Even if it means that we die the Apostles write in **Philippians 1:20, 24**- According to my earnest expectation and my hope, that in nothing I shall be ashamed, but that with all boldness, as always so now also Christ shall be magnified in my body, whether it be by life, or by death. For to me to live is Christ, and to die is gain.

But if I live in the flesh, this is the fruit of my labor: yet what I shall choose I know not. For I am in a strait between two, having a desire to depart, and to be with Christ; which is far better; Nevertheless, to abide in the flesh is more needful for you.

In this verse Paul was not just thinking about himself, but every person that was underneath him. When we allow God to be in control it won't matter when people are jealous of us, lie about us, or even backstab us. We must stay strong, and be determined to stand and stand on the wheel and not to let anyone make us jump off.

3 John 1: 2 Beloved, I wish above all things that thou mays prosper and be in Health, even as thy soul prospered. And the only way this can happen is we allow God to be in control of our lives.

When we pray and ask God to do things for us, we need to realize that God is in control, and He will do what He wants to do. We all are just a vessel for Him to use.

We get angry with God when He doesn't answer our prayers how we want. This is not something that godly people ever need to do. What makes us believe that we can command God? He can simply snap his finger, or just blow us away, and we are history.

I thought that I'd be finished with this book by now, but God said "No, I have other things that I want you to put in it. I want you to tell everyone about my goodness, and what I have done for you."

In the last few years my wife and I had gone through so many bad things. I began to think I wasn't in the will of God. He told me that He wants to use my wife and I to let people know that He was going to show and help people.

I've had three surgeries in the past five years. I've had plates put in my shoulders and neck, and had the removal of one of my kidneys. My wife had her gallbladder removed, had a mild heart attack, and suffered from breast cancer. Glory is to God that allows us to be here. We can to tell others that He is in charge, and He can do anything that He wants to do. He does not just test us, instead he allows us to be tested.

God wants people that He can use, people that are willing to go and stand on the Potter's wheel until He is finished. God wants someone that can share with others about how He can deliver us. We can't give up even when we are going through trials.

Sometimes we worry about our jobs, knowing that we need a better one. Some may say that they don't have enough money. Others say that they need a bigger house, so they can look better to other people. But as we read in **St. Luke 12: 15** which say unto them, take Heed, and beware of covetousness: for a man life consisted not in the abundance of the things which He possesses.

We see here that material things can cause you to get off the Potter's wheel. It isn't that something is wrong with material things, but you must be very careful that these things don't come between you and God.

We spend so much time trying to please mankind that we forget that we are here for the use of God. What is an abundant life? An abundant life is not how big your house is, or what job you have, or the amount of money you have in bank.

An abundant life is the relationship that you have with God. In **Philippians 4:19,** say, but my God will supply all your need according to his riches is glory by Christ Jesus. When we really get our self together and trust God we can see Him work out things in our live, and give us the things we need.

We must live a yielded life, and we must yield our life to God, so that He can have control over us. **Roman 6:10-13,** For in that He died, He died unto sin once: but He liveth unto God. Likewise, reckon ye also yourselves to be dead unto sin, but alive unto God through Jesus Christ our Lord.

Let not sin therefore reign in your mortal body, that ye should obey it in the lusts thereof. Neither yield ye your members as instruments unrighteousness unto sin: but yield yourselves unto God, as those that are alive from the dead, and your members as instruments of righteousness unto God.

Our Life is for service, Roman 12:1 I beseech you therefore, brethren, by the mercies of God, that ye present your bodies a living sacrifice, holy, acceptable unto God, which is your reasonable service.

And be not conformed to this world: but be ye transformed by the renewing of your mind, that ye may prove what is that good, and acceptable, and prefect, will of God. Our mind must be renewed every day.

We must be ready to go where God want us to go, and do what He wants us to do. Therefore, we must stay on the Potter's wheel.

When we stay on the Potter's wheel it means that we no longer want things to be our way, and that we are trusting on God to finish the work that He started in us, and become completed in his image.

We need to separate ourselves to serve God. **Roman 1:1** Paul a servant of Jesus Christ, called to be an apostle, **separated unto to the gospel of Gods.** Jesus has separated us from sin by his blood, and we are cleansed and sanctified unto righteousness.

Ephesians 5:18-20 And be not drunk with wine, wherein is excess; but be filled with the Spirit; Speaking to yourselves in psalms, hymn, and spiritual songs, singing and making melody in your Heart to the Lord; Giving thanks always for all things unto God and the Father in the name of our Lord Jesus Christ;

We must allow the Spirit of God to lead us, and teach us things that we need to grow, and be better than what we were yesterday. This is where we get our joy, peace, happiness, our love etc. Once we have these things going on in our lives then we go on to maturity.

1 Corinthians 13:11 When I was a child, I spoke as a child I understood as a child, I thought as a child: but when I became a man, I put away childish things.

1 Corinthians 3: 1, 2. And I, brethren, could not speak unto you as unto spiritual, but as unto carnal, even as unto babes in Christ. I have fed you with milk, and not with meat: for hitherto ye were not able to bear it, neither yet now are ye able. For ye are yet carnal: for whereas there is among you envying, and strife, and divisions, are ye not carnal, and walk as men.

When we can control these things then we can start eating meat because our teeth have grown and we can chew. Steak, chicken, pork chops, and all the other things that we eat to get our nutrition. **"We must allow God will to be done in our life"**.

In this life, we are faced with many things that come to us, and some of these things hurt badly. We must allow God to have his perfect will to be done even in all our pain.

Sometimes I wonder why God want us to go through these trials instead of just taking these away, so we don't hurt anymore.

These obstacles let us know that God is in control, and if we could fix ourselves it we would already been done. We ask the questions of "why this, and why that." Is it okay to question God? Our little children are killed; hate is running rapidly, love for many has become cold.

The biggest challenge that a Christian must face is fear. Fear has an attachment to us because of sin. We see evil and it makes us afraid. We go through trials, but we must learn, and must go through the process.

When we look in scripture we see how God always dealt with man because of fear. God always reminded man that He was in control of everything we are going through, and what we may face.

There are so many scriptures that apply to fear, I want to be able to present them all, but here I will only share a few in this chapter:

"After God delivered the children of Israel out of Egypt, he fed them and protected them. When they made it to the Red Sea fear came over them. They began to cry and complain to God that He brought them out of Egypt to be killed in the desert by the Egyptians."

God spoke through Moses to the children of Israel, **Exodus 14:13**, and Moses said unto the people, fear ye not, stand still, and ye shall the salvation of the Lord, which He will show to you today: for the Egyptians whom you see today, ye shall see them again no more for every.

When God fixes things for us and we are delivered we don't have to worry about them, or face them anymore. **I**

Samuel 17, Goliath of the Philistines of Gath, challenge Saul and the Israelite to see who would servants the other.

Fear rouse up in the Israelites, they did not know what to do, and they had forgotten what God had done for them in the past. Fear had them running around asking themselves "what are we are going to do now?" God always has a ram in the bush.

I Samuel 17: 45 Then said David to the Philistines, thou comest to me with a sword, and with a spear, and with a shield; but I come to thee in the name of the Lord of host, the God of the armies of Israel, whom thou hast defied.

This day will the Lord deliver thee into mine hand; and I will smite thee, and take thine Head from thee; and I will give the carcasses of the host of the Philistine fowls of the air, and to the wild beasts of the earth, that all the earth may know that there is a God in Israel.

If we trust God, even though we don't know what may happen, and allow his will be done in our lives then things will work out. He will get the glory. **II Corinthians 12: 7-9** And lest I should be exalted above measure through the abundance of the revelation, there was given tome a thorn in the flesh, the messenger of Satan to buffet me, lest I should be exalted above measure.

For this I besought the Lord thrice, that it might depart from me. And He said unto me, My grace is sufficient for thee: for my strength is made perfect in weakness. Sometimes we may feel that we as if we can't do anything or go any more, that when we relied on God, to give us the strength to go on to finish what He started in us.

Notes

Notes

Notes

4

What happens when you get off the Potter's Wheel?

We are to run and press toward the mark for the prize of the high calling of God, **Philippians 3:11-14** If by any means, I might attained unto the resurrection of the dead. Not as though I had already attained, either were already perfect: but I follow after, if that I may apprehend that for which also I am apprehended of Christ Jesus.

Brethren, I count not myself to have apprehended: but this one thing I do, forgetting those things which are behind, and reaching forth unto those things which are before I press toward the mark for the prize of the high calling of God in Christ Jesus.

Sometimes we start out well, but take our eyes off God. That is when we get off the wheel. We start looking at our circumstances, fall off the Potter's wheel, and then we begin to sin. People do things to us that we can't forgive, this causes bitterness to take root in our Heart, and sin sets in.

Hebrew 12:15, Looking diligently lest any man fail of the grace of God; lest any root of bitterness springing up trouble you, and thereby many be defiled; Lest there be any fornicator, or profane person, Esau, who for one morsel of meat sold his birthright.

When the roots of bitterness get in our heart it may cause us to be sick, and our physical body begins to have problems. The question asked by the Apostle Paul in book **Galatian 3:1-4** Foolish Galatians who hath bewitched you, that ye should not obey the truth, before whose eyes Jesus Christ hath been evidently set forth, crucified among you?

This only would I learn of you, received ye the spirit by the works of the law, or by the Hearing of faith? Are you so foolish? Having begun in the Spirit, are you now made perfect by the flesh?

When we look at things in the flesh we doubt the value of God's word. We only see the things that are in the physical world. We think that we don't have enough money, and we feel lust of the eye, lust of the flesh, and the pride of life.

We even look at our partners as if they don't care about us; saying they need another job because they aren't making enough. We even go as far to say the church is not doing anything! The real question is this: What are you doing?

These things happen when we get off the Potter's wheel and look to ourselves and allow our feelings to get in the way. Then we began to grieve the Holy Spirit, **Ephesians 4:30-32,** and grieve not the Holy Spirit of God whereby ye are sealed unto the day of redemption. Let all bitterness, and wrath, and anger and clamor, and evil speaking, be put away from you, with all malice: And be ye kind one to another, tenderhearted, forgiving one another, even as God for Christ's sake hath forgiven you.

A few years ago, before my mother passed away, so many things were going on. I had to stop and pray. It seemed as if my mother was pitting me and my siblings against each other. She would call one of us and tell us about what the other one was doing or saying, then call another sibling and do the same thing. So, I continued to pray unto the Lord and He shared with me that she was on the first stage of Alzheimer's disease.

If I had allowed those events to get to me and not stay on the Potter's wheel, I would have been defeated, and the Lord couldn't do what He wanted to do in my life. The purpose of staying on the wheel is to have victory in Christ Jesus.

James 1:2-8, my brethren, count it all joy when ye fall into divers temptation: knowing this that the trying of your faith worked patience, but let patience have Her perfect work, that ye may be perfect and entire, wanting nothing.

If any of you lack wisdom, let Him ask of God, that gives to all men liberally, and upbraided not and it shall be given Him. But let Him ask in faith, nothing wavering. For He that wavered is like a wave of the sea driven with the wind and tossed.

Getting off the Potter's wheel is like jumping off a train that is rolling down the track at 100 miles per hour! If it derails, it may have 200 cars behind it! You think to yourself, "Wow what a mess!" It takes a long time to clean up that kind of mess. What about the toxic waste that might be in some of the cars? That's what it will be like when we get off the Potter's wheel.

A few years ago, I got off the Potter's wheel, and made a big mess out of things while I was going through trials and tribulations. My wife and I went through a difficult time in our marriage when we were in North Carolina. At the church we attended, the pastor touched inappropriately. He was supposed to be my friend.

He tried to touch my wife like it was his duty to do so. I tried to talk to my wife after he did this to her, trying to let her know that what he did to her was the same as attacking me. She did not understand that I did not want to listen to what she was saying, because I felt so angry.

To me I felt it was like she was taking up for him, but I knew I was wrong. Therefore, you can't go on your feeling. I didn't realize that God was working out something in my life. I felt like someone dropped a ton of brick on top of us. I never got a chance to confront the pastor. The Devil was using this to get to me to jump off the Potter's wheel.

At one time, I felt like my wife betrayed me, because she didn't tell me what had happened. When I found out about it, I found myself yelling and screaming at her. I finally realized that she was afraid, and didn't really know what to do, but she thought she could trust Him and his wife.

There may be a couple that is going through something similar right now. Please, for God's sake don't let something like this hinder you from being the husband you can be. Love your wife, love your husband, and give each other the support that each of you need, even though you both may be hurting.

We have been trying recover from this madness, but I must confess that it has taken a long time to get this behind us. It hasn't been easy. I love my wife, and not only I was hurting, but she was hurting too. We as born-again men and women must do everything we can to protect our family, and love our spouse as much as Christ loves the church.

I messed up, so I want to be able to tell other people about how they need to dig down deep to forgive, and let go all of the junk. Otherwise, lots of people can be hurt behind things like this. I didn't do well at first, but now I see where I fell short. I need to be there for other people, so they don't go through what we went through.

Men, truly love your wife. Let her know that you really care. Please don't let pride get in the way, so you won't lose what you found. A man that found a wife found a good thing.

When we get off the Potter's wheel as a Christian, it doesn't mean we are not saved, however it does mean that when we make it to Heaven we may not have the reward that we deserve. Reward is for those of us that are saved, and we will be judge by this. We cannot work for salvation. Salvation is free, but we labor for the Lord to win souls for Him.

In the book of **James: 1:12-15** it talks about the crown

of life; blessed is the man that endured temptation: for when He is tried, He shall receive the crown of life, which the Lord hath promised to them that love Him. Let no man say when He is tempted, I am tempted of God: for God cannot be tempted with evil, neither tempted He any man.

But every man is tempted when He is drawn away of his own lust and enticed. Then when lust hath conceived, it brings forth sin: and sin, when it is finished, it brings forth death. So, brother and sister we may sin, but we must not practice sinning. When we get off the Potter's wheel we must get back on it quickly and ask God to forgive us that He may finish the work in our life.

In a family with children, as a parent we must allow God to teach us so we can teach our children. Everyone in the family from the mothers and fathers to the uncles and aunts must help the whole family.

God gives us the opportunity to get it right by allowing us to teach our children the things that will help them. We must get in the position to be able to hear what God is saying to us.

Proverbs 22:6, Train up a child in the way He should go: and when He is old, He will not depart from it. We are parent and we tell our children things, and sometimes we forget that they have a mind of their own.

So, we must back off, and let them make mistakes so they will learn, and remember they were trained up in the correct manner. Our children may not tell us about their mistakes, but they will remember what happened and what they learned.

When we accept the Lord in our lives that means that He is in control of us, and He will lead and guide us in the way we should go, and when we get old we will not depart from it.

Psalm 23:1 For the Lord is our shepherd and we shall not want, He maketh us to lie down in green pastures: He will lead us beside still waters. He restores our soul: He will lead us in the path or righteousness for His name sake.

Yes, although we walk through the valley of shadow of death, we will fear no evil, for He is with us; His rod and his staff will comfort us. He has prepared a table before us in the present of our enemies:

Then He anoints our Head with oil; He allow cup to run over. Surely goodness and mercy shall follow us all the days of our live: and we shall dwell in the house of the Lord for every.

St. Luke 9: 62, And Jesus unto them Him, no man, having put his hand to the plough, and looking back, is fit for the kingdom of God. Once you have taste the Lord you must not give up, and turn away from his goodness.

We may not understand why we may be going through things or why things are happening to us, we must stay on the Potter's wheel, and allow God to have the right away in our lives.

Notes

Notes

Notes

5

In Marriage do the right Thing

Marriage is honorable when the bed is undefiled, but whoremongers and adulterers will be judged by god. **Hebrews 13: 4**. When we go back to the beginning in the book of Genesis we see that God ordained marriage.

God performed the first marriage ceremony with Adam and Eve. **Geneses 2:18**, And the Lord God said, it is not good that the man should be alone; I will make Him a Help meet for Him.

This was the start of the family, God looked around and seen that every creature had a mate except for man, so He was created a woman for man. **Genesis 2:21-25**, And the Lord God caused a deep sleep to fall upon Adam, and he slept: and He took one of his ribs, and then closed up the flesh instead thereof;

And the rib, which the Lord God had taken from man, made Him a woman, and brought her unto the man. Not only did God make her but He introduces her to Him. Now Adam had a mate, a Wife.

And Adam said, "this is now bone of my bones, and flesh of my flesh: she shall be called woman, because she was taken out of man." Therefore, shall a man leave his father and his mother, and shall cleave unto his wife: and they shall be one flesh.

God placed man and his wife on the Potter's wheel but selfishness, disobedience, and hardness of the Heart came from Satan. These things cause man to stray away from what God required from Him. It takes a lot to stay on the Potter's wheel, but we must not let our feelings, or what someone says to us get us off the wheel.

If we stay on the wheel and wait on the Lord, we can see that it is a permanent bond that God wants for us. **St. Matthew 19:5, 6** And Jesus said for this cause shall a man leaves father and mother, and shall cleave to his wife: and they shall be one flesh.

Wherefore they are no more twain, but one flesh. What therefore God hath joined together let not man put asunder.

In these times, Christian men and women you don't want to back down, from things that happen to us, that don't mean that you are soft, it just means you are going to stay on the wheel.

You see we just must stay and understand God is in control and He wants the best for us so we can be a witness for Him.

Ephesians 5: 22-30, Wives submit yourselves unto your own husband, as unto the Lord. For the Husband is the Head of the wife, even as Christ is the Head of the church: and He is the savior of the body.

Oftentimes a woman thinks that they are nothing compared to their husband. Or she believes that he trying to get over on her. Instead, take the time and look to see what God wants to do in your life to work things out.

The wife was taken out of man's side to be a Help Meet. She meets the needs of her husband, but is not a door mat. She helps make the family strong. She must realize that she is on the Potter's wheel, and God is trying to make her a better wife.

Therefore, as the church is subject unto Christ, so are wives to be subject to their husband in everything. Husband, love your wife, as Christ also loved the church, and gave His life for it.

We sometime forget as man just how much Christ love the church. We must learn to love our wives just as much regardless of what we think, or what they have done. The only way this can happen if we stay on the wheel and allow Jesus take control of our lives.

Sex and **money** are the two biggest things that cause problem in a marriage. If if a man is not making enough money, the wife gets afraid and thinks that he not doing enough.

A woman wants a man that makes lots of money. If he isn't making the kind of money that she thinks he could make, then she doesn't love him. The wife needs to love him for who he is, not and what he brings home. Maybe that is all he can do at the current time. They need to learn to love Him because money will soon depart.

In whatever the job or how much money he is making, hang in there. Love him, and pray that God will provide for the both of you. Wife is the man's Help Meet. That means that you need to work together to stay on the Potter's wheel, so God can get the glory out of your lives. That is what a Help meet is to do. Don't ridicule your husband because of money, that will make him feel like less of a man, and he will not want to do anything.

Issue number two is sex. This is the biggest thing in marriage break up, because one or the other feels that they are not getting enough sex. I am trying to learn how to be more intimate with my wife. Sometimes all you have to do is listen to your partner.

If you haven't been taught how to be intimate, then how or what would you know what to do, say, or feel? Sex plays a big important role in a marriage.

1 Corinthians 7:5 Defraud ye not one the other, except it be with consent for a time, that ye may give yours to fasting and prayer, and come together again, that Satan tempt you not for your incontinency.

Satan loves when husband and wife fight over not having enough sex. He will cause one or the other to stray, and want to be with someone else.

<u>Forgiveness</u> is one of the things we must learn how to do, and we can't do it ourselves. It takes the blood of Jesus, and not jumping off the Potter's wheel. If say we are Christian and we get off the Potter's wheel, how can we share with the world that God is in our lives?

We must read and study God's word and see what He is saying to us, and not look to the world to give us the answer.

St. Matthew 5:13-16 Ye are the salt of the earth: but if salt have lost his savor, wherewith shall it be salted?

It is thenceforth good for nothing, but to cast out, and to be trodden under foot of men. Ye are the light of the world a city that set on a hill that can't not be hid, neither do men light a candle, and put it under a bushel, but on a candlestick; and it giveth light unto all that are in the house.

Let your light shine before men, that they may see your good works, and glorify your Father which is in Heaven. Husband and wife must learn how to forgive each other; this is the process that God requires from his people.

A few years ago, my wife and I went through a very hard time. We thought that the pastor that we were under was our friend. He touched her inappropriately and she didn't tell me for a year. When I found out about it, this almost destroyed our marriage. The distrust, Lies, deceitfulness, hurt all these things began to come up in our live.

We straggled to get our marriage back to where it was, but through all of that I have learned that if you don't trust God and stay on the Potter's wheel you will allow the Devil to destroy you.

I had lots of anger, bitterness, and hate in my Heart. I was not realizing that as I was holding on to negativity, it was destroying me. Sickness came in my body; I was being suffocating in my sin.

When I was in Theology College getting my Doctoral degree, I studied about being in bondage. This is what was happening to me. I was in bondage and didn't realize this what was going on with me.

You see, it isn't the big sin that we miss. It's the little things that keep us in bondage. The tiny things will cause us not to grow in the grace of God. We need to change our thinking about what God want us to do, and grow so we can help other.

My sister told me that I must do the right thing, and what was the right thing? I started looking at myself, praying and asking God to forgive me. This helped me getting back on the Potter's wheel. I realize that this struggle was not really about me, but that God wanted to get the glory out of my life.

Sometimes when we allow ourselves to get in the way of our own lives, we get off the Potter's wheel, but God is faithful enough to reach down and pull us back. We must ask Him to forgive us, and really repent.

There was layer of sin like an onion that God began to pull back in my life, things that he wanted me to see. These things hurt, but I thank God for grace, and that He loves me enough to let me see these things and work them out of my life.

There are lots of Christians people that are in bondage and don't know what to do escape. We must learn to study, read, and stay in God Word so we can grow.

St. Luke 8: 4-11, And when much people were gathered together, and were come to Him out of every city, He spoke by a parable: A sower went out to sow his seed: and as He sowed, some fell by the way side; and it was trodden down, and the fowls of the air devoured it.

Some fell upon a rock; and as soon as it sprung up, it withered away, because it lacked moisture. And some fell among thorns; and the thorns sprang up with it, and choked it.

And other fell on good ground, and sprang up and bear fruit a hundredfold. And when He had said these things, He cried, He that hath ears to hear, let Him hear. And the disciples asked Him, saying, what might this parable be?

And He said, unto you it is given to know the mysteries of the kingdom of God: but too other in parables; that seeing they might not see, and Hearing they might not understand.

Now the parable is this: The seed is the word of God. Those by the way side are they that Hear; then cometh the devil, and taketh away the word out of their Hearts, lest they should believe and be saved.

They on the rock are they, which, when they Hear, receive the word with joy; and these have no root, which for a while believe, and in time of temptation fall away. And that which fell among thorns are they, which when they have Heard, go forth, and are choked with cares and riches and pleasures of this life, and bring no fruit to perfection.

But that on the good ground are they, which in an honest and good Heart, having Heard the word, keep it, and bring forth fruit with patience.

I have been working on these things for a few years, and I guess God isn't finished with me yet. Every day it's like an onion being peeled. He continues to show me more of myself. These are things in my life that He wants me to get rid of so I can be completed.

I have been praying for something for about twenty years and, He just recently opened the door for me to do it. I learned that it wasn't time for me to do it; I had to stay on the Potter's wheel and wait for God open the door. If we can just hold on and not get into a big hurry, but trust God He will do what He said He would do.

Notes

Notes

Notes

6

Don't let anyone or anything's push you off the Potter's wheel

When we go to the beginning of time, we see that God made man (Adam) and then made woman (Eve). **Genesis 3:1-6** it was then when the serpent came to Eve and said yea, hath God said, ye shall not eat of every tree of the garden? And the woman said unto the serpent, we may eat of the fruit of the trees of garden:

But of the fruit of the tree which is in the midst of the garden, God hath said, ye shall not eat of it, neither shall ye touch it, lest ye die. And the serpent said unto the woman, ye shall not surely die:

For God doth know that in the day ye eat thereof, then your eyes shall be open and ye shall be as gods, knowing good and evil.

And when the woman saw that it the tree was good for food, and that it was pleasant to the eyes, and a tree to be desired to make one wise, she took of the fruit thereof, and did eat and gave to Her husband and He did eat.

This was the first time that man jumped off the Potter's wheel. We always want to do what we want to do, instead of hearing what God has said.

Satan quoted scripture to Eve but, did not tell the whole truth about how wants to get us off the Potter's wheel. He knows how to use others to get his work done. So, we need to be prepared and know what the word of God is saying to us.

Satan will use anyone to deceive us. God told Abram that He was going to bless Him with a son but, Sarai didn't believe. So, he had Abram to sleep with her maid **Genesis 16:3.**

Genesis 27:1-27 We see that Rebekah, Jacob's mother caused Him to fall off the Potter's wheel. She had Him to lie to Isaac, her husband so she could steal Esau's blessing.

Falling off the Potter's wheel is like a big rock going down a steep hill. It picks up speed as it goes downhill.

Genesis 29:1-35 Jacob had to run away after falling off the Potter's wheel, after lying to his father and stole his brother birth right. His brother wanted to kill Him.

We must stay focused on the Lord, and continue to read and pray so we won't get trick by Satan. As you look in the Bible we see how some of God's people aren't focused. They allow others to make them fall, or they just give up themselves and jump off.

Joseph was focused on God, but he went about tell his brother things in the wrong way about his dream, but he was still focused. His was about hated, but he still stayed on the Potter's wheel.

They didn't like all the truth that he would tell. They eventually hated him, and sold him to the Ishmeelites. When they had brought Him to Egypt there, he was tested and was in prison under Potiphar for 20 years. **Genesis chapter 38-39.**

David was the beloved of God after killing Goliath and fighting the Philistines. You'd think that he had it made forever. God anointed him before he was king, but because of King Saul's jealousy, David had to run for his life. He had to stay on the Potter's wheel for a few years before he took over as king of Israel.

Even though He was God's beloved He still got off the Potter's wheel, when He committed adultery with

Bathsheba. Not only did that make him a murderer of her husband Uriah, he lied and tried to cover up his sin.

God is merciful if we just learn to ask him to forgive us our sin, and get back on the Potter's wheel so He can finish making us. When we fall off we think that God is out to get us **"Repent"**. In actuality when we repent, God will forgive us, no matter what it is if we are true. We must also be godly in our sorrow.

2 Corinthians 7:10, for godly sorrow worked repentance to salvation not to be repented of: but the sorrow of the world worked death. **2 Peter 3:9**, the Lord is not slack concerning his promise, as men count slackness, but is longsuffering to us-ward, not willing that any should perish, but that all should come to repentance.

Don't let anyone tell you that don't have to do all of that. We need to always ask for forgiveness, and then forgive each other. We must keep ourselves clear so God can use us for his glory and it's not how we feel.

Sometimes the way people act, or what they say may or will cause us to jump off the Potter's wheel, or we just fall off because we have given up. Your life is important, so don't let anything or anyone push you off.

God so loved the world that He gave his only begotten son. Whosoever believed in Him should not perish, but have every lasting life **St. John 3:16**.

We need to be careful who we are around and who we talk to. It can be so easy to get side tracked. Everybody that says that they love you isn't honest, and sometimes you must watch those so-called friends. They are the ones that will try to take you down when things are going well.

In 2015, I wanted to be finished with this book and have is published by now, but God said "No! I have a different plan for you." In January 2016 of this year, I passed out at home. My wife told me that I stopped breathing, and could not find a pulse. She thought I was going to die. A call to an EMT was done, but by the time they got to our home I was up and was feeling ok.

They insisted that I go to the hospital and get checked out. I was ok and didn't think It was necessary to go to the hospital, but said ok anyway. While in the hospital they ran all kind of tests for my blood, gave me x-rays and CT scans. They could not find reason for me to pass out, but they looked closely and found a mass on my right kidney. It turned out to be cancer.

My kidney was removed because the doctor didn't want to take a chance with just cutting the mass and leaving part of the cancer in. Glory is to God through Jesus Christ, for he blessed me on that day. God is so amazing to have given Doctor the wisdom to do the things that they do.

Notes

Notes

Notes

7

Feeling Can get in the of staying on the Potter's wheel

L iving for God is not how we feel. Feeling has gotten in way of many people's ability to serve God. Our feelings change like the wind, they go in a direction way one minute, and another direction in another minute. Sometimes our feelings go up and sometimes they go down.

We can't allow our feelings to come in when we are trying to service the Lord, so we can't put God on the back burner and then tell ourselves we will pick him up later.

When Jesus was facing the cross he didn't say, "Well that doesn't look so good, or I don't want to go on the cross for them. So, I will go away until next year and come back and maybe I will feel like it then. We are serving the Lord so we need to stay on the Potter's wheel until God get finished.

St. Mark, 14:32-38 and they came to a place which was named Geth-sem'-a-ne: and He sayeth to his disciples, sit ye here, while I shall pray. And He taketh with Him Peter and James and John, and began to be sore amazed, and to be very heavy; and said unto them, my soul is exceeding sorrowful unto death: tarry ye Here, and watch.

And He went forward a little, and fell on the ground, and prayed that, if it were possible, the hour might pass from Him. And He said, Abba, Father, all things are possible unto thee; take away this cup from me: nevertheless, not what I will, but what thou wilt.

And He cometh, and fined them sleeping, and said unto Peter, Simon, sleeps thou? Couldest not thou watch one hour?

Feeling refers to subjective reactions, pleasurable or unpleasurable, that one may have to a situation. They can be from an absence of reasoning or a lack of trust my own emotions. Emotion implies an intense feeling with physical as well mental manifestations.

Feeling is the full nature of expressing emotion and sensitivity; with sympathetic senses by which sensations of contact, pressure, temperature, and pain are transmitted through the skin. Our sense of touch is a part of our consciousness. The plural definition of feeling there are several nouns that described feeling sense of touch, is as such the sense of touch of when you are touching something's. It is the ability to have a physical sensation in a part of your body.

Something experienced physically or mentally is, something felt emotionally is as perceived as emotionally states. Affection is the response of love, sympathy, or tenderness toward somebody. The ability to express emotion or impression sensed is an impression, appearance, effect, or atmosphere sensed from something.

Instinctive awareness is having a feeling that something is going to happen before it happens. There are many expressions that can be considered if we go on our feeling, and since God is a Spirit we must worship Him in spirit and in truth.

When we're going through things and don't know how we got where we're at, we must take time to stop and pray. We have to do this so we may know what God's will is. Don't let anyone, anything, or your feeling get you off the Potter's wheel!

Sometimes, someone or something might make us feel like we are not important, or make us feel that we are nothing. Don't let anything or our feeling get in the way of staying on the Potter's wheel.

There are many things that people say to us that can shake us up or make us slip; our emotions are something that we work on for our entire lives. In marriage, we must be aware of our feelings, because it will cause break-ups, divorces, and you may never recover from it.

It is so important that we teach our children about their feelings so when they grow-up and leave home they want get caught up in their emotions.

Notes

Notes

Notes

8

No Condemnation

When we ask God to forgive us and truly mean it in our hearts, sometimes it is hard to forgive ourselves. We must ask God to forgive us, and then find in our heart to forgive ourselves. When God forgives us, we must find a way to reach deep down in our heart to forgive our self.

Roman 8:1-2 there is therefore now no condemnation to them who belong to Christ Jesus, for this is power of the life-giving if we don't walk after the flesh, but after the Spirit. For the law of the Spirit is life in Christ Jesus hath made us free from the law of sin and death.t to come into our life. Because the law of Moses could not save us, because of our sinful nature.

We must never allow the devil trick us, and try to bring

back in our mind something that we did before we allow Christ into our Heart.

James 4:6, 7 But He giveth more grace. Wherefore He said, God resisted the proud, but giveth grace unto the humble. Submit yourselves therefore to God. Resist the devil, and He will flee from you.

Sometimes things happen to us in our lives that we can't control, yet some things can be controlled. What exactly do we do? We can't change things that we have no control over. We need to let them go, because if we could have fixed it, we would have done it before we go through it.

We can't let material things control us or cause us to get off the Potter's wheel, we must let it go.

Philippians 3:13-15, Brethren, I count not myself to have apprehended: but this one thing I so, forgetting those things which are behind, and reaching forth unto those things which are before.

I press toward the mark for the prize of the high calling of God in Christ Jesus. Let us therefore, as many as be perfect, be thus minded: and if in anything ye be otherwise minded, God shall reveal even this unto you.

When we stumble off the Potter's wheel, God expects us to get up and dust ourselves off. He doesn't want us to stay in the mess that we got ourselves into. That is the reason why he allows things to come our way for us to be strong, so we can help someone else.

Sometimes we're in situations where we don't know which way to go. We pick the wrong road, or read a sign that says one thing and we make it out for something else.

We must get back on the right road, and get back on the Potter's wheel so God can finish the work He started in us. Sometimes people think that God is the one causing their suffering. God allows Satan to take us through things to make us strong, but we must stay in the word of God.

I Corinthians 10:13, There hath no temptation taken you but such as is common to man: but God is faithful, who will not suffer you to be tempted above that ye are able; but will with the temptation also make a way to escape, that ye may be able to bear it.

The flesh is always getting into trouble and we need to be able to control it.

St. Matthew 26:41, Watch and pray, that ye enter not into temptation: the spirit indeed is willing, but the flesh is weak. We see in this scripture Jesus is teaching the disciple we must watch and pray.

We may fall, stumble, or say something that we shouldn't say to a person, but we need to find the path where we need to be. We will realize just how much God loves us and that he has save us.

It is not about how much people will forgive us. Instead, it is how much we will forgive other, and ourselves. This is because there is no condemnation to Him that is in Jesus Christ. If we don't forgive each other or ourselves, Satan will try to make us jump off the Potter's wheel.

2 Corinthians 5:17, 18 If any man be in Christ, he is a new creature; Old things are passed away; behold, all things are become new, all things are of God, who hath reconciled us to Himself by Jesus Christ, and hath given to us the ministry of reconciliation.

Trials and tribulations come to make us strong. We may lose some battles, and win others, but we can always remember the battle is not ours, it belongs to the Lord.

1 **Samuel 17: 45-47**, then said David to the Philistine, Thou comest to with a sword, and with a spear, and with and shield:

But I come to thee in the name of the Lord of host, the God of the armies of Israel, whom thou hast defied. This day will the Lord deliver thee into mine hand; and will smite thee, and take thine Head from thee; and I will give the carcasses of the host of the Phili'-tines this day unto the fowls of the air, and to the wild beasts of the earth, that all the earth may know that there is a god in Israel.

And all this assembles shall know that the Lord saveth not with sword and spear; for the battle is the Lord's, and He will give you into our hands.

The Lord already knows what we are going through, and that He will make a way for us. All we need to do is stay on the Potter's wheel to have the victory. Sometimes people try to make us feel like we have done something wrong. They may even say "You're supposed to be saved," trying to make us feel guilty. Satan will use anything and anyone to make us feel condemned. Remember, we don't go on our feelings; they will get us in trouble every time.

St. John 8:34-37, Jesus answered them, Verily, verily, I say unto you, whosoever committeth sin is the servant of sin. And the servant abideth not in the house for ever: but the Son abideth ever. If the Son therefore shall make you free, ye shall be free indeed.

One of the tricks that the devil uses is to make us feel guilt about our past, even trying to make us feel like we aren't saved. If you accept Christ in your life and you believe in your heart and confess with your mouth that Jesus is Lord, then you are saved, and the Devil can't do anything about it.

Notes

Notes

Notes

9

Stand Firm on the Potter's Wheel

Sometimes the Bible is misunderstood. We read it and get the wrong understanding of what is being said, and then receive the wrong interpretation. Satan comes along and brings confusion.

We must remember that confusion is not of God, it comes from Satan. He will do whatever he can, to keep us from standing on the Potter's wheel. God wants us to have the full understanding so we can stand firm on his Word.

Galatian 5:1 Stand fast therefore in the liberty wherewith Christ has made us free, and be not entangled again with the yoke of bandage. The things that **God** deliver us from He doesn't want us to go back to them. He doesn't want us to look back at them but, to go forward.

If we ever decide to go back God scripture let us know what it is like if we go back or turn away in.

Proverbs 27:10,11 The great God that formed all things both rewarded the fool, and rewarded transgressors. As a dog returned to his vomit, so a fool return to his folly.

Genesis 19: 17, 24-26, And it came to pass, when they had brought them forth abroad, that He said, escape for thy life; look not behind thee, neither stay thou in all the plain; escape to the mountain, lest thou be consumed.

God never lets anything slip by him. We may not know what is going on, or even what is happening, let alone understand at times. That is the why we need to stay on the Potter's wheel. You must put all of your faith in God.

Then the Lord rained brimstone and fire upon Sodom and upon Gomorrah. He overthrew those cities, and all the plains, and all the inhabitants of the cities, and that which grew upon the ground.

But Lot's wife looked back, and she became a pillar of salt. No, I don't believe we will turn into a pillar of salt, but our lives will lose the value when we go back to the old things before we came to the Lord. We must stand on the **Word of God** for its full value.

When we go through things and times get hard, we must remember that the flesh will cause us to miss out on the good things that God has in store for us. Even the ones that are closest to us can cause us to miss out if we are not careful.

We must learn how to give God the glory even when we are going through suffering. After all, He is the one making us better each day. God gets the glory out of our lives even when we are going through trials.

2 Corinthians 12:1-10 Apostle Paul teaches here how when things are not going the way that we desire, we must look to God because his grace is sufficient for us. We learn when we are weak, that is God that makes us strong. When we go through our infirmities, God gets the glory and He gets all the praise from us. This is what makes us strong.

We must stand on the word of God to help us make it through these things, so we can be a blessing to someone else. Our lives aren't just for us. They're also for others, so they can see how God can work anyone through bad situations. This is the reason that we make sure that we stand firm on the Potter's wheel.

When we hear the Word of God and He speaks through his word we must apply it to our lives, and set the example for others.

Ecclesiastes 9:11, I returned, and saw under the sun, that the race is not too swift, battle to the strong, neither yet bread to the wise, nor yet riches to men of understanding, nor yet favor to men of skill; but time and chance happened to them all.

Habakkuk 2:1-4 I will stand upon my watch, and set me upon the tower, and will watch to see what He will say unto me, and what I shall answer when I am reproved. And the Lord answered me, and said, write the vision, and make it plain upon tables, that He may run that reads it.

For the vision is yet for an appointed time, but at the end it shall speak, and not lie: though it tarry, wait for it; because it will surely come, it will not tarry. Behold, his soul which is lifted up is not upright in Him; but the just shall live by his faith.

God gives us an appointed time to do His will. When we receive it or hear it we must be ready to run and share with others so they will be able to see what God wanted them to do. We are the just, and shall live by the faith that He has given us to do so.

Notes

Notes

Notes

10

When we get off the Potter's Wheel (Moral Value Decreases)

Proverbs 14: 27-35, the fear of the Lord is a fountain of life, to depart from the snares of death. In the multitude of the people is the king's honor: but in the want of people is the destruction of the prince.

He that is slow to wrath is of great understanding: but He that is hasty of spirit exalted folly. A sound Heart is the life of the flesh: but envy the rottenness of the bones.

He that oppresses the poor reproaches his maker: but He that honored Him hath mercy on the poor. The wicked is driven away in his wickedness: but the righteous hath hope in his death.

Wisdom rested in the Heart of Him that hath understanding: but that which is in the midst of fools is made known. Righteousness exalted a nation: but sin is a reproach to any people.

The king's favor is toward a wise servant: but his wrath is against Him that causes shame. **Proverbs 11:11**, by the blessing of the upright the city is exalted: but it is overthrown by the mouth of the wicked.

There are some bosses out there that don't treat their employees with respect. If you are out there and reading this book, you must show respect to get respect. Treat your employees' right.

When I was in the seventh grade, my science teacher gave my class a word of wisdom. He told us that if we were working a job and found a better paying job, sometimes the old boss will want to persuade us to stay by offering more money. Don't take it, because they could have paid you more at the start.

What does it mean to have morals? As time go on we see that our moral values have decreased and the love of many has become cold. Let's look at what it means to be a moral person:

When we look at the definition of moral we see that it is how a person relates to the principles of rules, conduct, and distinguishes between right and wrong.

When we look back in history, every country that forgot about morals failed. They allowed their thinking to take over instead of doing the right thing

2 Chronicles 7:14 If my people, which is call by my name, shall humble themselves, and pray, and seek my face, and turn from their wicked ways; then will I Hear from havens, and will forgive their sin, and will Heal their land.

There are lots of people today are saying they are God people. I am talking about born again Baptist who believe in Jesus.

St. John 3: 1-12, There was a man of the Pharisees named Nicodemus, a ruler of the Jews.

The battle starts first in our mind and, we must be ready to fight this battle. We are in a spiritual war and must have on armor of God to be a winner.

Ephesians 6:10-18; finally, my brethren, be strong in the Lord and in the power of his might. Put on the whole armor of God that ye may able to stand against the cunning devices (wiles) of the devil.

For we wrestle not against flesh and blood, but against principalities, against powers, against the rules of darkness of this world, against spiritual wickedness in high places. We see that the battle started in our mind.

This is what the devil uses to confuse us, thinking that it is someone other than ourselves. Yes, then we blame God for things that go wrong in our lives instead of looking for the true problem.

Young people don't have respect for their elders, and they talk to them any kind of way. Children disrespect parents.

2 Timothy 3:1-7 this know also, that in the last day's perilous times shall come. For men, shall be lovers of their own selves, covetous, boasters, proud, blasphemers, disobedient to parents, unthankful, unholy,

Without natural affection, trucebreakers, false accusers, incontinent, fierce, despisers of those that are good, Traitors, Heady, high minded, lovers of pleasures more than lovers of God; having a form of godliness, but denying the power thereof: from such turn, away.

For of this sort are they which creep into houses, and lead captive silly women laden with sins, led away with diver's lusts.

The government has played a big role in breaking up the home. It has told the women if you don't have the man in the home we will give you free money. So, they don't have the right man in the home there for the children. These children don't have a solid structure to be raised with.

Therefore, this whole generation will be lost because of this. Then only God will be able to straight it out if the Lord hasn't returned.

Notes

Notes

Notes

Conclusion

Many people have all difference though about what God will do, or their idea about what is happening. We are living in the last days and the Lord is coming back for his people.

We must be ready when he come. Lots of people want God to line up with what they think or say, it doesn't work that way. We must line up with God and his Word.

Whether you are rich or poor you will stand before God and give account of the dead that you've done in this body. **I Peter 4:17,** For the time is come that judgment must begin at the house of God: and if first begin at us, what shall the end be of them that obey not the gospel of God?

Ecclesiastes 12: 9-14, And moreover, because the preacher was wise, he still taught the people knowledge;

yea, he gave good heed, and sought out, and set in order many proverbs.

The preacher sought to find out acceptable words: and that which was written was upright, even words of truth. The words of the wise are as goads, and as nails fastened by masters of assemblies, which are given from one shepherd.

And further, by these, my son, be admonished: of making many books there is no end; and much study is a weariness of flesh.

Let us hear the conclusion of the whole matter; **Fear God, and Keep his commandments: for this is the whole duty of man.**

For God shall bring every work into judgment, with every secret thing, whether it be good, or whether it be Evil.

Matthew 12: 36, But I say unto you, that every idle word that men shall speak, they shall give account thereof in the day of judgment. For by thy words thou shall be justified, and by thy words thou shalt be condemned.

About the Author

In 1954 born into this world David Allen (Garmon) Jordan Sr. Born in Hayti, Missouri, son of Willie C. Garmon who was a share cropper and my mother Almeda "Davis" Garmon, worked chopping and picking cotton. Today I am grown God fearing preacher that preach and teach.

I've learned how to stand on the Word of God and listen to what "He" God is telling me in the Spirit. It's still a spiritual battle warfare. Through many ups and down, fall, and failure I have learn to stand on the promises of God, and to stay on the potter wheel.

I met my beautiful wife Carla, we got marry in 1993 in St. Louis Missouri and move to North Caroline where we reside for 11 years and have three beautiful children.

My son David Jr. when he was born weights 2 pound 12 ounces, God began to use me to stand not on what I knew, but what he was doing in my life. My wife and I had some hard time in our marriage, and if not for the hand of God moving in our life and standing on the potter wheel, we wouldn't be together today.

While we may have going through things in our life, with the up and down we were learning how we must stand on the potter wheel and not jump off. Because we trusting in God, he made ways out of nothing for us.

God bless Carla and I with four beautiful daughters, Cosandra, LaTisha, Myra Alexandria, and Michala Grace, and two handsome son Joshua, David Jr, They all has been an inspiration and a blessing to me.

I believe that God has directed me to write this book so other could be help by hearing my testimony, and how God have brought us out.

We were made in the image of God and he want the best for us. So, to understand what ours part is we must read and study God word and pray. The main things are to stand on the potter wheel and don't jump off.

CPSIA information can be obtained
at www.ICGtesting.com
Printed in the USA
BVOW06*0905141217
502785BV00005B/6/P

9 781973 606918